Jeremy Jennings joined the staff of Holy Trinity Brompton (HTB) in 1985 and started a weekly prayer meeting there in 1990, which is still running today. The corporate prayer at HTB grew into an activity involving hundreds of people under Jeremy's leadership and he still helps lead HTB's weekly prayer meeting. His other book, *The Church On Its Knees*, is about how to develop and run prayer in the local church and was published in 1998. Jeremy has spoken at prayer conferences nationally and internationally and he and his wife now live in West Sussex.

THE
PRAYER
OF
GOD

Reflections on the Lord's Prayer

JEREMY JENNINGS

Matador
9 Priory Business Park,
Wistow Road, Kibworth Beauchamp,
Leicestershire. LE8 0RX
Tel: 0116 279 2299
Email: books@troubador.co.uk
Web: www.troubador.co.uk/matador
Twitter: @matadorbooks

ISBN 978 1800463 455

British Library Cataloguing in Publication Data.
A catalogue record for this book is available from the British Library.

Typeset in 11pt Adobe Garamond Pro by Troubador Publishing Ltd, Leicester, UK

Matador is an imprint of Troubador Publishing Ltd

I am hugely indebted to Mark and Amanda Elsdon-Dew, whose encouragement and professional support were invaluable throughout the production of this manuscript. I also want to thank Bishop Sandy Millar for all his input including the provision of two of the illustrations used. Then there has been the long-term support of our pastors Nicky and Pippa Gumbel and, before them, Sandy and Annette Millar, who epitomise encouragement for which I am forever grateful. I also want to express how much I owe to the many people at Holy Trinity Brompton with whom I have spent hundreds of hours praying at all kinds of prayer meetings and events. Thank you, too, to Pete Greig and Mike Andrea and all our other friends at 24-7 Prayer. Last but not least, Milly – you have lovingly supported me through so much including this latest effort.

It has been so great to journey with you all.

DEDICATED TO THE AUTHOR AND
PERFECTER OF OUR FAITH

Contents

1

The Prayer of God

THE LORD'S PRAYER

The Lord's Prayer is at the epicentre of Christianity. It has been taught by parents to their children for the best part of two thousand years. Practically every Christian in the world knows it by heart. It is a dearly loved part of our heritage and culture. It remains perfect and current, unique and irreplaceable. It is iconic and powerful. I love the Lord's Prayer!

Given in answer to a request from one of the disciples, 'Lord, teach us to pray…' (Luke 11:1), it links us to the prayer life of its author. It also forms part of Jesus' teaching in the Sermon on the Mount as recorded in chapter six of Matthew's Gospel.

Of course, it is possible to say the prayer by rote and I have often done that in the past. But it has been gaining meaning and significance in my life more recently. For example, sometimes I pray it when I am awake during the night. I have then been taking the time to dwell on each section, trying to get more deeply into the meaning, like spending time with a good friend.

You find all of life is covered in this short prayer. It has been a journey but one where it is almost better to travel than to arrive. It has been like a conversation with God and, at times, it brings such a sense of his closeness and peace. The direct link to Jesus makes it even more special and I have found by praying this prayer in such a way you get to know him better.

However, it is also a prayer for change. It opens the door to worship, provision, forgiveness, protection and so much else. It boldly proclaims the rule and reign of God and it confronts evil. It draws us to the Holy Spirit and the presence of God. 'Your kingdom come' has been at the heart of every prayer meeting I have led. There is power in the Lord's Prayer and we should use it to the full.

My background is not in theology or teaching – I have written the pages that follow as one of this extraordinary prayer's users. The Lord's Prayer is a prayer for all time and every season. Here it is in the form used throughout this book:

Our Father in heaven,
Hallowed be your name,
Your kingdom come, your will be done,
On earth as in heaven.
Give us today our daily bread.
Forgive us our sins as we forgive those who sin against us.
Lead us not into temptation but deliver us from evil.
For the kingdom, the power and the glory are yours now and forever.
Amen

2

The Family of God

OUR FATHER IN HEAVEN

When we write a letter we need the name and address of the person we are writing to. In the Lord's Prayer, Jesus gives us both in the opening line. Right from the start of the prayer, we are like children approaching our father but a far better father than we have ever known, our Father in heaven.

We enter a world of belonging and security based on the love of the Father. Paul put it like this, 'For this reason I kneel before the Father…' (Ephesians 3:14) acknowledging that he is the head of the family of which we are a part.

When Jesus was baptised a voice from heaven said, 'This is my Son, whom I love; with him I am well pleased' (Matthew 3:17). The first four words of the Lord's Prayer bring the assurance that we belong to the same family. I once sensed God saying during a time of corporate prayer, 'You have my ear', and I believe that is true every time a child of God begins to pray as Jesus taught.

So, this uniquely great prayer starts with the word 'Father' and to pray it effectively we need to understand that it is, in this sense, the Christian family prayer. We also need to understand that this parent is in heaven and is the God who created the heavens and the earth. Those closest to him never stop saying, 'Holy, holy, holy is the Lord God Almighty, who was, and is, and is to come' (Revelation 4:8). So he is indescribably holy but approachable, all powerful but loving and he is forever but now.

As for heaven, we know that it is God's home and the Bible gives various partial descriptions of it, all of which are breathtaking. But heaven is also where God is and I love the description of a future time when he has come to dwell with his people, where 'He will wipe every tear from their eyes. There will be no more death or mourning or crying or pain, for the old order of things has passed away' (Revelation 21:4). Whatever else it is, heaven is a place of kindness and love.

When Jesus answered the question, 'Lord, teach us to pray...' (Luke 11:1), he revealed what we need to know to enter his world of prayer with the words, 'Our Father in heaven'.

*

It was one day in the spring of 1972 that my faith came alive. Having been encouraged by my young wife and some good friends for several months to do so, I finally knelt on my own and surrendered my life to Jesus. I remember asking his forgiveness for the things I had done wrong and took a step of faith that he was 'there'. He was and it changed my life. That day I experienced God as 'Father' and joined a family that has Father, Son and Holy Spirit at its head, heart and centre. It is one I am still so proud to belong to.

PRAYER: Thank you that we belong to your family and heaven is where you are…

FOR CONSIDERATION:

1. Are you comfortable relating to God as 'Father'?
2. How do you imagine heaven?
3. How do you feel about God living with his people one day (see Revelation 21:3)?

3

The Name of God

Names are important and the name of God is no exception. The fuller meaning of the word 'name' here extends to wider aspects of God's greatness. This includes his nature and character as well as 'the power and the glory' that the Lord's Prayer acknowledges later. Accordingly, the word has a vast reach in the context.

The Concise Oxford Dictionary defines 'hallow' as 'honour as holy'. As Christians, we long for the day when God is honoured more widely, and 'Hallowed be your name' expresses that strong desire as a prayer. However, as we pray it we also find we are joining with the worship of heaven. It is not as if we can add to God's holiness as that is already complete. But it is that we can celebrate it. We can begin to glimpse his beauty and perfection and give glory, honour and thanks in the process. Someone once asked me if the worship in our prayer meetings was just 'padding'. I hope my reply was polite but it is at the very heart of the activity!

Many, if not all, of the great prayers in the Bible include

praise. For example, there is a prayer in Acts which begins, 'Sovereign Lord, you made the heaven and the earth and the sea, and everything in them' (Acts 4:24). The prayer continues with more praise and then intercession before the passage concludes, 'After they prayed, the place where they were meeting was shaken. And they were all filled with the Holy Spirit and spoke the word of God boldly' (Acts 4:31). It was a dramatic turnaround with praise being an important part of the prayer concerned.

God's name was considered too holy for the Old Testament people to pronounce but Jesus taught us to say 'Father'. At a stroke, that opens the door to intimacy and access but we must hold this in tension with the reverence that the greatness of God deserves. His name is to be treated as absolutely holy because he is absolutely holy.

*

It is customary to stand for the Hallelujah Chorus during Handel's *Messiah*. There is a tradition that this began on 23 March 1743 when King George II stood for it at the London premiere. Because he was the king, everyone else had to stand too! The chorus reaches its crescendo:

> 'And he shall reign forever and ever,
> King of kings forever and ever!
> Hallelujah! Hallelujah!
> And Lord of lords forever and ever!'

It's a wonderful picture of one king leading his subjects in the worship of the 'King of kings'!

PRAYER: Give us fresh glimpses of your holiness and greatness as we pray 'Hallowed be your name'...

FOR CONSIDERATION:

1. How do you address God in your prayers?
2. Do you include praise and thanksgiving in your prayers?
3. Do you regard God as approachable?

4

The Kingdom of God

YOUR KINGDOM COME

'Your kingdom come' is a prayer, a hope and a battle cry. Jesus began the reconquest of this fallen, suffering world during his life here and left his followers to carry on the struggle, which will end with final and total victory when he returns. Sometimes defined as God's rule and reign, we need to understand that his kingdom is opposed in the here and now. It is a spiritual kingdom and the opposition is spiritual. Paul says, 'For our struggle is not against flesh and blood, but against the rulers, against the authorities, against the powers of this dark world and against the spiritual forces of evil in the heavenly realms' (Ephesians 6:12).

The trouble is that these unseen spiritual forces lie behind so much of the suffering we see through the likes of poverty and injustice, corruption, oppression, starvation and sickness. Every time we pray, 'Your kingdom come', it engages us in the struggle for a better world. However, the kingdom also 'comes' when we as individuals surrender stubborn areas in our own lives to the will of God, often with some difficulty but always with beneficial results in the long run.

The kingdom of God is diametrically opposed to the forces of darkness and this line in the Lord's Prayer aligns us with the will of God. Make no mistake, the struggle is real. Jesus put it like this, 'From the days of John the Baptist until now, the kingdom of heaven has been forcefully advancing, and violent people have been raiding it' (Matthew 11:12). The very language puts us on notice of the reality of the contest. It is said that Satan trembles at the sight of the weakest saint on their knees. When asked about spiritual warfare, I always say that prayer is an important part of it.

Ultimately, the battle is for the hearts, minds and souls of people. Speaking of God, Paul says, 'For he has rescued us from the dominion of darkness and brought us into the kingdom of the Son he loves, in whom we have redemption, the forgiveness of sins' (Colossians 1:13-14). New disciples bring growth and life to churches and much benefit to the local communities they serve. The kingdom comes at the expense of the dominion of darkness and, as a Christian, you are on the front line. However, though there may be battles, always remember you are on the winning side.

When we pray, 'Your kingdom come', we are crying out for forgiveness, salvation and healing through the cross of Christ for lost and broken lives and a lost and broken world. Therefore, it is at the very heart of Jesus' mission to save the world and we are looking forward to that wonderful day when the king returns and his kingdom is fully consummated.

*

There is no doubt that the kingdom of God advanced powerfully during the life of John Wesley. He recorded in his journal how he reluctantly went to a meeting in Aldersgate Street, London, on 24 May 1738 and listened to a sermon. During it, his heart became 'strangely warmed'[1] and he found a new trust in Christ as saviour. He went on to found the Methodist movement and to change the course of English history through his ministry. It is estimated he rode over 250,000 miles and preached more than 40,000 sermons during his career! Like so many others down the ages, he made Jesus his king and prayed and worked tirelessly for the advancement of his kingdom.

PRAYER: Show your power and release your kingdom…

FOR CONSIDERATION:

1. How would you describe the kingdom of God?
2. What are we looking for when we pray, 'Your kingdom come'?
3. How has Jesus made joining this kingdom possible?

---

1 John Wesley, *The Journal of John Wesley* (F. H. Revell, 1903; independently published 2016), p. 56.

5

The Will of God

YOUR WILL BE DONE ON EARTH
AS IN HEAVEN

The fulfilment of this line in the Lord's Prayer was to cost Jesus his life. Praying in the garden of Gethsemane, he said, 'My Father, if it is possible, may this cup be taken from me. Yet not as I will, but as you will' (Matthew 26:39). He embodied the answer to his own prayer and went to the crucifixion having prevailed in the unimaginable struggle that took place on that fateful night in the garden.

Obedience lies at the very heart of the Christian faith and most of us will remember a time or times when we have had to surrender our wills to the will of God. Jesus said, 'If you love me, keep my commands' (John 14:15). The extraordinary thing is that this is the place of victory for us.

To walk away from a wrong relationship, to break a bad habit, to tell the truth, or even to pursue a new path, may be hard but, if we are following God's will, it will always lead to freedom in the end. The phrase about God, 'whose service is perfect freedom', puts the conundrum so well. Heaven would not be heaven if the will of God was not done there. It follows that 'earth' becomes more like heaven as his will is done here.

Ironically, the Christian army is the only one that finds victory on its knees. I was watching the News one night and an article from *The Sunday Telegraph* was featured. It was about the decline in church attendance and so on under the heading, 'The Church on its knees'. But when I saw it, the thought that immediately flashed into my mind was, 'That's not the problem, it's the solution!'

The Church on its knees depicts it in prayer and surrendered to the will of God. Once we are there, all things are possible. We need to remember that in Jesus' life the crucifixion was followed by the resurrection, when history was forever changed. To pray, 'Your will be done', and mean it, whatever the cost, is about as powerful as it gets. But never forget that God has your best interests at heart and is a good God.

*

One evening, a young man approached our vicar Sandy Millar at the end of a service in the London church Holy Trinity Brompton. He explained that he wanted to give his life to the Lord but had been wrestling with all the things he supposed he would have to give up. Towards the end of the worship, he had sensed a voice saying, 'Why don't you give in and we'll both win?' His question was, 'Do you think that could be God?' Sandy replied, 'Well, do you know anyone else who would let you think you had won if you had given in?' After a moment's thought, he replied, 'No, I don't think so', and gave his life to the Lord.

PRAYER: Help us to put your will first…

FOR CONSIDERATION:

1. How do we know the will of God?
2. Has there been a time when you have had to adjust your will to align it with the will of God?
3. Do you think kneeling in prayer is necessary and/or helpful?

6

The Provision of God

GIVE US TODAY OUR DAILY BREAD

Jesus lived in an agrarian economy and 'bread' would have been essential to most people's existence. As such, it can be seen as representing the basic needs of life in this line of the Lord's Prayer.

Someone told me about a successful man who, in later life, liked to remind his children that they could only eat one meal and they could only wear one suit or outfit at a time. No matter how much you may have, the fundamental needs of life relate to shelter, clothing, food and health. Jesus said, 'So do not worry, saying, "What shall we eat?" or "What shall we drink?" or "What shall we wear?"' (Matthew 6:31). The list is quite a short one!

A key word in this section of the Lord's Prayer is 'daily'. Although saving, such as for retirement, is generally a good thing, this is not so much about storing up provision for the future as it is about trusting God to provide for our needs as they arise. Our 'daily bread' may come through a job or other source of income but we ought always to remember that all we have comes from God. We depend on him as the giver of earth, rain, sun, seed and so much else, for all provision and life itself. Even though we talk about someone as a 'breadwinner', who provides for themselves and their family, our ultimate dependence on God remains.

I once sensed God saying in a moment of financial anxiety, 'You will always have enough'. It was so reassuring and 'Give us today our daily bread' also reminds us to give thanks for what we are given.

Although the prayer for 'bread' clearly relates to us and our families, it also has a wider application. Many people do not have somewhere to live, do not know where their next meal is coming from, cannot afford adequate clothing or do not have access to good healthcare, and this line in the Lord's Prayer also applies to them. We live in a world where many are in food poverty and we see the need for food banks all around. In this sense, this part of the prayer is a plea for the reduction of poverty and its effects. As we pray, we may even find we want to become part of the solution by taking action or giving.

Jesus said, 'But seek first his kingdom and his righteousness, and all these things will be given to you as well' (Matthew 6:33). Our material needs matter to God and he promises to provide as we make his kingdom and righteousness our priority. It is also good to remember that he has the power of miraculous provision.

*

George Muller (1805–1898) ran orphanages in Bristol where thousands of children were cared for over the years.

One morning, there was no food in the larder and no money to buy any. The children were waiting for their breakfast and Muller prayed, 'Dear Father, we thank you for what you are going to give us to eat'. Then came a knock at the door and it was the baker, who said, 'I felt in the night you didn't have any bread for breakfast so I have baked some and here it is'. No sooner had he left than there was a second knock at the door and it was the milkman. He said his milk cart had broken down right in front of the orphanage and he would like to give the children his load of milk!

PRAYER: Thank you for your provision... and today we pray for...

FOR CONSIDERATION:

1. What are some of your 'daily' needs?
2. Are you comfortable praying for your own needs?
3. How have you experienced God's provision?

7

The Forgiveness of God

FORGIVE US OUR SINS AS WE FORGIVE THOSE WHO SIN AGAINST US

The Bible is blunt. It tells us, 'If we claim to be without sin, we deceive ourselves and the truth is not in us' (1 John 1:8). We all need forgiveness and it is obtained through the cross of Christ. The Christian life begins with repentance. On that day in 1972, I knelt and prayed a simple prayer to Jesus in which I asked for forgiveness and surrendered my life to him. It was very tentative at the time but from that moment everything changed. Before then I knew *about* Jesus, afterwards I knew *him*. I understood he had died for me. His salvation is the greatest gift I have ever received.

Naturally, being human, I have often found myself asking for forgiveness since but it has always been in the context of the relationship with God that started in 1972. I have never doubted his love for me through all the ups and downs and have found his promise is true: 'Never will I leave you; never will I forsake you' (Hebrews 13:5). Having reminded us that we are all sinful, the Bible goes on to say,

'If we confess our sins, he is faithful and just and will forgive us our sins and purify us from all unrighteousness' (1 John 1:9). To know you are forgiven by God is the most wonderful experience – like a heavy load being lifted off you.

However, 'Forgive us our sins as we forgive those who sin against us' is structured to include our forgiveness of others. Jesus put it like this, 'For if you forgive other people when they sin against you, your heavenly Father will also forgive you. But if you do not forgive others their sins, your Father will not forgive your sins' (Matthew 6:14-15). To forgive those concerned is a basic requirement if we want to be forgiven by God.

Of course, there are degrees of sin and some sins are more easily forgiven. But sometimes the action of others can inflict deep wounds. The debt is real. In the criminal realm, we yield the responsibility to administer justice to the state but even that does not remove all responsibility from us as we still have to forgive. We serve a Lord who, as he was hanging on the cross, asked God to forgive his executioners. The bar is set very high. When Peter asked Jesus whether he should forgive someone up to seven times, Jesus told him to forgive without limit.

The trouble with unforgiveness is that it diminishes us and will end up defining us. To understand that forgiveness sets us free, and does not depend on the response we get, is transformational. Once we see that, we can embrace it more easily. 'Forgive us our sins as we forgive those who sin against us' may be one of the most challenging lines in the Lord's Prayer but it is also one of the most liberating ones, so long as we live by it.

*

On 8 November 1987, during the Northern Ireland troubles, Marie Wilson, then a twenty-year-old nurse, was killed when the IRA detonated a bomb during the Remembrance Day parade at Enniskillen. Later that evening, her father Gordon, who had held her hand as she died, was asked by a news reporter what he thought of the men who planted the bomb. Gordon, who had a strong Christian faith, replied, 'I bear no ill will. I bear no grudge'. He later spoke of how he forgave the bombers and would pray for them. This has been described as a turning point in the IRA's campaign of violence.

PRAYER: Forgive us for...and help us to forgive...

FOR CONSIDERATION:

1. What difference has God's forgiveness made to you?
2. How do you correlate being forgiven with forgiving others?
3. Why is it so important to forgive?

8

The Protection of God

LEAD US NOT INTO TEMPTATION BUT DELIVER US FROM EVIL

Jesus is the only person who has never sinned. Described as one who 'has been tempted in every way, just as we are – yet he did not sin' (Hebrews 4:15), he is the only person never to buckle under the weight of temptation. It is not a sin to be tempted because Jesus faced that, 'yet he did not sin'. The issue is how we handle the process and the outcome. 'Lead us not into temptation' shows us we can appeal to God for help when we need it.

Of course, the word 'tempt' can properly convey the sense of 'to test' as in to try the resolution of someone, as well as being an enticement to sin. Abraham endured a test of obedience on Mount Moriah with Isaac and passed, after which God promised him enormous blessing as a result. When we started a new prayer meeting at our church, we ran into a real test of opposition. In the end, after prayer, God intervened and the meeting became established and grew. The thing about this kind of testing is that you emerge stronger afterwards. God may test us from time to time but he will never tempt us to sin.

However, the Lord's Prayer is realistic and it portrays a power of evil in this world. 'Deliver us from evil' is better understood as 'Deliver us from the evil one'. William Barclay puts it like this, 'The Bible does not think of evil as an abstract principle or force, but as an active, personal power in opposition to God'. So when 'Jesus was led by the Spirit into the wilderness to be tempted by the devil' (Matthew 4:1), God saw it as a test in the good sense but the devil saw an opportunity to tempt him to sin. As we know, Jesus passed the test and went on to fulfil his mission 'in the power of the Spirit' (Luke 4:14), and the devil failed in his.

We need to be realistic. The Bible says, 'Your enemy the devil prowls around like a roaring lion looking for someone to devour' (1 Peter 5:8). He uses the weapon of temptation and to fall into a pattern of persistent sin is a very destructive place in which to find ourselves. A friend told me that, when he was a young associate pastor, his senior pastor warned him to watch out in three areas: money, sex and alcohol. Of course, these are fine in the right context but they can also become snares. Whilst the list may vary a little, it is wise to be on your guard in the areas concerned.

Naturally, God's forgiveness is available at any stage if we repent but nipping things in the bud is the wiser course of action. It is always encouraging to remember that, '…God is faithful; he will not let you be tempted beyond what you can bear. But when you are tempted, he will also provide a way out so that you can endure it' (1 Corinthians 10:13).

To look the other way can save a load of grief. President Garfield of the United States was once presented with a financially attractive but morally dubious proposition in the wrapper 'No one will ever know'. His answer was, 'President Garfield will know and I've got to sleep with him!' The force of temptation to sin is real but one of our main defences is to think of the damage a wrong course of action could inflict. To bring the Lord into disrepute is to be feared at all costs, even before we consider the consequences to our churches, families, friends and ourselves.

Jesus knew the struggle against temptation and he taught us to pray, 'Lead us not into temptation but deliver us from evil'. We should follow the Lord and seek God's protection when it comes to temptation and evil.

*

The Nobel Prize winner, Aleksandr Solzhenitsyn (1918-2008), was imprisoned for eight years for criticising Stalin. In his work *The Gulag Archipelago* he wrote, 'The line separating good and evil passes not through states, nor between classes, nor between political parties either…but right through every human heart…and through all human hearts. This line shifts. Inside us, it oscillates with the years. And even within hearts overwhelmed by evil, one small bridgehead of good is retained'.[2] Needless to say, with God's help, it's a line we definitely want to remain on the right side of at all costs.

---

2   Aleksandr Solzhenitsyn, *The Gulag Archipelago 1918–1956* (Abridged Edition, Vintage Classics, 2018), p. 312.

PRAYER: Protect us from temptation…and from the attack of dark forces…

FOR CONSIDERATION:

1. How do you know when you are being tempted?
2. Have you experienced being tested with a positive outcome?
3. How do you understand evil?

9

The Glory of God

FOR THE KINGDOM, THE POWER AND THE GLORY ARE YOURS NOW AND FOREVER

This section of the Lord's Prayer is an addition to the Biblical version and as a result not all parts of the Church include it. However, countless people down the ages have learned it and the prayer accordingly seems somehow incomplete without, 'For the kingdom, the power, and the glory are yours now and forever'. It is a doxology or expression of praise to God and a grand final note to end on.

It draws to mind the awesome power of God in a way that confirms the validity of the rest of the Lord's Prayer. When I close a prayer meeting, I often say, 'Thank you for praying, you have made a difference'. But I also sometimes say during a meeting, 'Who do we think we are; what difference can we possibly be making?' However, I would always then go on to say, 'The issue is not who *we* are but who *he* is – the one who is listening to our prayers'. That's the point!

This line in the Lord's Prayer very much points us to God's glory. We may get a glimpse of that through some glorious aspect of creation like the Alps in Europe, or through a spectacular building like St Paul's Cathedral in London, or from a wonderful painting or something else but this can only be incomplete at best.

We can also see something of God's glory through the Transfiguration. When the disciples heard the voice of God on that occasion '…they fell face down to the ground, terrified' (Matthew 17:6). On another occasion, after Moses had asked of God, 'Now show me your glory' (Exodus 33:18), he was told, 'I will cause all my goodness to pass in front of you…But you cannot see my face, for no one may see me and live' (Exodus 33:19-20), and he was only allowed to see God's back.

God's glory is unimaginable and unsurpassable. The twenty-four elders who surround his throne in heaven '… fall down before him who sits on the throne and worship him who lives for ever and ever. They lay their crowns before the throne and say: "You are worthy, our Lord and God, to receive glory and honour and power, for you created all things, and by your will they were created and have their being"' (Revelation 4: 10-11). One day, there will surely be many other crowns lying there as well.

The fullness of God's glory can never be known in this life. However, it is good to be reminded of it and the doxology in the Lord's Prayer does that.

*

I believe the Lord once said to me, 'Empty church buildings bring me no glory'. An archdeacon in the Church of England said on another occasion, 'An empty church is like the palace of a long-forgotten king…' So, what a great way to glorify God in the 'now' of the doxology, to pray and work for churches full of Christians who then start new ones which also fill and do the same again! In due course, we will all be able to join in the 'and forever' dimension too.

PRAYER: Now show us your glory…

FOR CONSIDERATION:

1. What reminds you of God's glory?
2. Is God restrained in the use of his power?
3. How can we bring glory to God?

10

The Power of God

'COME HOLY SPIRIT'

In Luke's Gospel, Jesus' teaching on prayer culminates with an encouragement to ask God for the Holy Spirit. It seems as if that was always the target destination, and he travels a careful route to reach it.

We are told, 'One day Jesus was praying in a certain place. When he finished, one of his disciples said to him, "Lord, teach us to pray…"' (Luke 11:1). I thank God for that disciple! It seems reasonable to think that the underlying dynamic to the request was that he had seen enough of Jesus' answers to prayer to be very keen to learn more about the way he prayed. Imagine witnessing the feeding of the five thousand!

In response, Jesus gave him the words that we know as the Lord's Prayer. That then flowed into an extraordinary story about a man getting some bread from his friend at midnight through sheer persistence. It was clearly not a very welcome request given that the friend's door was firmly locked and he was in bed, but the outcome was successful! Jesus is not comparing God to a reluctant friend – quite the reverse, but he is making a clear point about the approach we should adopt when it comes to prayer.

He continues this emphasis on persistence: 'So I say to you: ask and it will be given to you; seek and you will find; knock and the door will be opened to you' (Luke 11:9). The same theme re-occurs in the Parable of the Persistent Widow where we are told, 'Then Jesus told his disciples a parable to show them that they should always pray and not give up' (Luke 18:1). Again, he is not comparing God to an unjust judge but he is reinforcing the need to prevail in prayer in the face of opposition.

He then reassures the disciples that they can trust God to respond with goodness and kindness with a very human illustration: 'Which of you fathers, if your son asks for a fish, will give him a snake instead? Or if he asks for an egg, will give him a scorpion?' (Luke 11: 11-12).

Jesus concludes by saying, 'If you then, though you are evil, know how to give good gifts to your children, how much more will your Father in heaven give the Holy Spirit to those who ask him!' (Luke 11:13). The age-old prayer of the Church is 'Come Holy Spirit'. We receive the Spirit by asking, with persistence if necessary, whilst holding onto Jesus' promise, 'For everyone who asks receives…' (Luke 11:10).

In my experience, we don't 'do' life or church very well without the Holy Spirit. Asking for the Spirit is a constant cry of our prayer meetings. Why? Because the Church needs power to accomplish its mission and Jesus said, 'But you will receive power when the Holy Spirit comes on you; and you will be my witnesses…to the ends of the earth' (Acts 1:8). On the day of Pentecost that power came and it is still available today. The Great Commission would be 'mission impossible' without the Holy Spirit.

It is therefore so important to make space for the Spirit in our lives and churches. In my own life, I experienced being 'filled' by the Holy Spirit when someone prayed for me and I now ask God for more of the Spirit on a regular basis. C. H. Spurgeon said that is necessary because we 'leak'! I would always try and do this before doing something like leading a prayer meeting, but it is equally important in all walks of life, in business, in acting and so on. After all, Jesus promised the Spirit to be with us and we all need his help and strength in the challenges we face.

Part of an effective Christian life also includes allowing the 'fruit of the Spirit' to grow, '… the fruit of the Spirit is love, joy, peace, forbearance, kindness, goodness, faithfulness, gentleness and self-control' (Galatians 5:22). We see in Jesus a life where the 'power' and the 'fruit' of the Spirit were perfectly combined and, suffice to say, we need both as well.

To pray 'Come Holy Spirit' in a church service or meeting and to wait should always be dynamic. I have heard so many stories of God moving powerfully in such times and it can be life changing. If you are leading, it may take courage to wait but it is always worthwhile. It is said, 'All good things come to those who wait', and that is certainly true of the Holy Spirit. The ultimate answer to the Lord's Prayer, and indeed to all prayer, is the Holy Spirit who brings the presence and power of God and that opens the door to the realm of healing, miracles and all the other gifts of the Spirit.

*

On one occasion, my friend Sandy Millar was leading a time of prayer at an Alpha conference in Sheffield, England. He had asked the Holy Spirit to come and fill the delegates as they stood and waited. Whilst often the presence of the Spirit is evident by the reaction of those present, on this occasion little appeared to be happening. After what seemed a long time as he kept privately asking the Lord to bless those involved, Sandy felt the Lord saying, 'These are my sheep and I am ministering to them'. He closed the meeting for lunch quite shortly afterwards, a little disappointed with the response. After the conference, however, he had more letters than ever saying, 'You will never know but this is what the Lord did…' It is always right to trust God when it comes to the prayer 'Come Holy Spirit'.

PRAYER: Come Holy Spirit…

FOR CONSIDERATION:

1. How do we receive the Holy Spirit?
2. What difference does the Holy Spirit make in our lives?
3. What difference does the Holy Spirit make in our churches?

Appendix

Here is a prayer, based on some of the sections of the Lord's Prayer, for anyone who would like to start or reconfirm a relationship with God:

FORGIVE US OUR SINS

Father, I am sorry for the things I have done wrong in my life... Please forgive me and help me make a fresh start. I now turn from the things that I know have been wrong.

HALLOWED BE YOUR NAME

Thank you Jesus that you died on the cross for me so that I could be forgiven and set free. I now ask for that forgiveness.

YOUR KINGDOM COME

Holy Spirit, please come into my life, fill me and lead me from this day forward.

OUR FATHER IN HEAVEN

Thank you that I can call you 'Father' and belong to your family.

AMEN

If you prayed this prayer, how exciting! The best thing to do now is:

1. Tell a Christian friend and/or
2. Find a good introductory course to the Christian faith like Alpha and/or
3. Join a church where you feel at home.

 **Matador**

For exclusive discounts on Matador titles,
sign up to our occasional newsletter at
troubador.co.uk/bookshop

Lightning Source UK Ltd.
Milton Keynes UK
UKHW022152200221
379054UK00005B/115

9 781800 463455